Motor Racing at

Nassau

in the 1950s & 1960s

Terry O'Neil

$12.94 + $3.55

VELOCE PUBLISHING
THE PUBLISHER OF FINE AUTOMOTIVE BOOKS

Those were the days ...

www.veloce.co.uk

First published in October 2008 by Veloce Publishing Limited, 33 Trinity Street, Dorchester DT1 1TT, England. Fax 01305 268864/e-mail info@veloce.co.uk/web www.veloce.co.uk or www.velocebooks.com.
ISBN: 978-1-84584-198-0/UPC: 6-36847-04198-4

Contents

Acknowledgements & Foreword.. 4

1954 – First races at Windsor Field 7

1955 – Consolidation 15

1956 – Final races at Windsor Field.. 19

1957 – A move to Oakes Field.... 22

1958 – Oakes Course; a change of direction. 27

1959 – Politics and racing... 35

1960 – Single seat racing, Formula Junior.. 43

1961 – Two for Dan Gurney 47

1962 – Lotus XIX stranglehold.. 54

1963 – American muscle 62

1964 – Penske's year 69

1965 – Foreseeing the future 77

1966 – The final scene 85

      Summary of winners 91

Index 95

Acknowledgements & Foreword

Acknowledgements

I am greatly indebted to a number of people who helped me with the composition of the text for the Bahamas Speed Weeks book, published in 2006. Whilst this book covers the same thirteen years of racing, it does so in much more of a pictorial fashion, though enough text has been included so as to give the outline to the story. Therefore, I once again acknowledge the contributions of, in no particular order: George Waltman, Willem Oosthoek, Michael Lynch, David Seielstad and Denise McCluggage for providing information towards the written work.

Also, importantly, my thanks go to John Owen, Ted Walker, Tim Hendley, Alexis Callier, Patsy Kenedy Bolling, Michael Eaton, Roy Schechter, Roland Rose, and Ted Cianfrani for generously allowing me to use a large proportion of the photographs that appear in this book.

Foreword

Opportunism played a part in the establishment of racing at Nassau in the Bahamas. Situated about 160 miles off the Florida Coast of America the, then, British colony was as strongly influenced by what went on in America as by British rule. Its geographical proximity to Florida gave easy access to Americans, and it was one in particular who seized upon the opportunity to introduce motor-racing under the banner of the Bahamas Speed Weeks. His name was Sherman 'Red' Crise.

Sherman Crise was a keen sailor and, in 1953, whilst on one of his frequent visits to Nassau with his

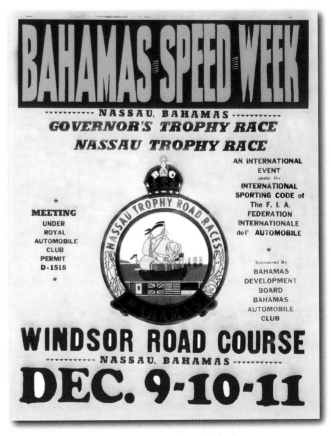

1954 poster produced by the Speed Weeks organisers.
(Courtesy George Waltman)

wife Evelyn, had made a mental note of the wide expanse of disused runway at Windsor airfield which could mirror existing racing locations being used in America. At the time, a joint programme of events was being organised and run between the Sports Car Club of America and Strategic Air Command whereby races were held at military airfields in America. In addition to those races, others were being planned and run at civil airports throughout America on a smaller scale.

Crise was no stranger to motor racing as, before WW II, he had organised a number of half-mile track events for midget cars that ran on alcohol and caster oil. While initially their popularity was not that great, the idea caught on and tracks sprang up all over America, the largest of which was at Hershey Park where Crise was born. WW II put an end to Crise's organisational activities but this potential opportunity to re-establish himself as an organiser was too good to miss. He decided to contact a number of businessmen in Nassau to see if they would be interested in forming a joint venture with him in establishing the old Windsor airfield site into a race circuit, where a series of races could be held on an annual basis. The meetings with two people in particular, Sir Sydney Oakes and Robert Hallam Symonette, who were both members of the Nassau Development Board, produced a positive response and as a first step towards achieving their aspirations, they formed a motor club. Known as the Bahamas Automobile Club, it had Sherman Crise as Chairman with the other committee members being Sir Sydney Oakes, Robert Hallam Symonette and Charles Jane.

Before any thought of arranging a motor race could be made, the newly formed club needed approval from the Royal Automobile Club in London and the American Automobile Association, as well as permission from the authorities in local government to use the facilities at Windsor Field. All parties approached gave approval to the plans put forward: no doubt having Sir Sydney Oaks and Robert Symonette as members of the Nassau Development Board helped the cause.

While it might have appeared an easy task to achieve their aims it really was not that simple. In 1954 the Bahamas had a truly divided society. There was the white community from where many of the businessmen came, known locally as the 'Bay Street Boys.' It wielded a great deal of power, both in financial and political terms. Then there was the black and coloured communities which between them could barely muster an opposition party and had little or no say in the running of the Bahamas. Needless to say the latter had no influence in the formation of the Speed Weeks or any of the arrangements that surrounded the events. Indeed, as time went on, there was voluble discord within the black community as it forcefully argued that monies spent on the Speed Weeks could have been better put to use in providing hospitals and schools.

There was also an issue with having American members of the Sports Car Club of America enter the races. The SCCA enjoyed an amateur status so its members were unable to accept prize money or payment in kind. The SCCA pointed out to its members that, should they accept an invitation to attend the Speed Weeks event in the form presented to them, then they would be in violation of SCCA rules and, as such, would be expelled from the Club. The Bahamas Automobile Club countered this statement by arguing that those rules only prevailed on US soil, and as the Bahamas was under British jurisdiction, the American drivers could take payment as they did for racing in Europe. All of this debate became academic in 1959 as the growth in professionalism within motor racing had given the SCCA no option other than to accept that it had to change its stance on prize money.

With true optimism planning went ahead for the first event to be held in December of 1954. The organisers had won the backing of the authorities in the Bahamas, they being swayed by the promise of the economic benefits that would accrue from the influx of Americans to the Bahamas to watch the races.

Looked at from the perspective of the people who came to compete in the races, the Speed Weeks offered an opportunity to enjoy a relaxing period of up to ten days of socialising, racing and attending parties. For many the social aspects were as important as the racing, for each night one or more of the island's splendid hotels played host to a cocktail party. Weather permitting, the receptions were held outdoors where the kaleidoscope of brightly coloured bougainvillea, perfumed rose mallow, the moonlight shining through the tall palm trees, a shimmering swimming pool, calypso music and the muffled sound of the surf breaking on the beaches blended to make the occasions memorable. After the parties had finally finished and the free drinks had disappeared, groups of people gathered in the hotel bars, or would venture further afield to a district called 'Over the Hill.' The area had small bars and eating places that were somewhat more private than the official venues used by the organisers. Many are the unsubstantiated stories of competitors seen staggering out of a nightclub or bar back to an hotel just in time for breakfast, a shower, then down to the track to compete in a race. It certainly gave credence to the idea that the local economy was reaping the benefit of the Speed Weeks.

The one aspect of the races that the organisers never managed to achieve was that of having accurate entry lists and result tables. While they tried to update the entry lists to the best of their ability, the entrants would sometimes bring a different car to the event than the one originally entered. It goes a long way towards explaining why the printed programme would vary from the cars in the actual starting line-up for some of the races. Consequently the race reports varied depending on the knowledge and diligence of the journalist at the event, the race entry issue he had to hand at the time, and finally the state he or she was in following the parties of the night before ...

1954
First races at
Windsor Field

The end of a busy and somewhat traumatic SCCA race season in America had come and gone by the time the invitations to attend the Speed Weeks had hit the mailboxes of those who had expressed an interest in attending the 1954 event. It was maybe no surprise that many of the top named drivers chose not to attend after a busy season, but in all, 60 applications were accepted by the organisers to practise their driving skills around the Windsor Field 3.5 mile course, described by some drivers as a nightmare. Little or no work had been carried out to improve the broken and overgrown highly abrasive surface of

1954 programme cover.
(Terry O'Neil Collection)

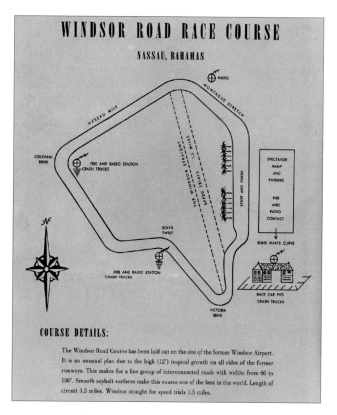

Map of Windsor Field. (Terry O'Neil Collection)

the runways at Windsor which, made from crushed coral rock and asphalt, was very hard on tyre wear. Of those people invited to enter the races, it was decided by the organising committee that a proportion were to be local drivers as it was thought prudent to have local interest in the races.

Apart from the local cars, the majority of the vehicles were shipped to Nassau from Miami aboard the SS Queen of Nassau as part of the package deal, while a

1954 - First races at Windsor Field

few other cars came direct from New York on the SS Lapland. On arrival at the port in Nassau, the cars were first driven to the British Colonial Hotel where many of the participants were staying, then paraded down Bay Street on their way to be housed in disused hangers adjoining Windsor Field, as there were no covered pits at the track.

Having housed their cars, the entrants were then at liberty to enjoy the varied and generous hospitality offered as part of their overall package by the organisers of the Speed Weeks.

Drivers' overall badge. (Terry O'Neil Collection)

Jaguar cars represented the largest single marque present at Nassau, even out numbering the MGs in attendance. Burns #70 was one of the more unfortunate Jaguar drivers, failing to finish in the Nassau Trophy Race in his XK120M specification car. (R Rose. Terry O'Neil Collection)

Voluntary helpers were a crucial part of the Speed Weeks. The Bahamas police force gave assistance with crowd control (not too arduous a task!) while Crise had sought the assistance of Charles MacDonald of the American Automobile Association to do the race timing with electronic gadgetry recently used at Utah Salt Flats.
(R Rose. Terry O'Neil Collection)

Local Bahamians were invited to join in the fun at Nassau. A special Residents' Race had been arranged for which there were 14 entrants. The race was won by Juan Fernandez driving an Austin-Healey 100, while the Singer 1500 driven by David Lowe finished in 10th position overall. (R Rose. Terry O'Neil Collection)

Erwin Goldschmidt had gained fame with his driving exploits in an Allard J2X but had the opportunity of purchasing a Ferrari 375 Plus. Maglioli had recently driven this Ferrari factory-entered car in the Carrera Panamericana Race in Mexico, then it was shipped out to Nassau for Goldschmidt. The Carrera Panamericana Race had obviously taken its toll on the car as Goldschmidt found to his cost, as he had to replace a broken steering rod after practising in the car. (R Rose. Terry O'Neil Collection)

It may appear disorganised, but everyone knew their place on the Tarmac where they could park and attend to their car. The Americans were now used to racing at airfields and usually came well prepared for the elements, in this case, the fierce sun. Were they safe from passing cars? Well, that was another matter. (George Waltman. Terry O'Neil Collection)

Sir Sydney Oakes may have been part of the organising committee but he was not above giving a helping hand, and is seen here in the check shirt doing flag duty during one of the races. (R Rose. Terry O'Neil Collection)

The races were organised on the same basis that SCCA races in America were run, with four main categories of cars divided into Classes dependant on engine size. Once established, it allowed the organisers to 'mix and match' the Classes so as to form as many races as they saw fit to run. The one exception to the rule was for the Resident's Race, where all cars irrespective of Class were run together.

1954 was the only year that included motorcycle races. They were run prior to the car events and, so far

After finishing a very satisfying and successful season in America, Candy Poole brought his Crosley-powered PBX to Nassau. It was usually entered in Class HM but was included within Class G at Nassau due to lack of other Class HM cars. It didn't stop him from continuing his winning streak as he won Class G in the Bahamas Automobile Cup ahead of some larger capacity cars.
(David Ash Archive, courtesy Michael Eaton)

A rare colour photo taken of Sir Sydney Oakes, one of the people on the organising committee of the Speed Weeks. Although he was a popular man, he was never quite as popular as his beautiful Danish wife, Greta. Greta managed to captivate everyone with her charms, added to which she was quite a good driver. (David Ash Archive, courtesy Michael Eaton).

David Ash was a prominent member of the MG Car Club in America and brought his MG TF to Nassau to represent the marque. For a car more adept on tighter courses it struggled to make any lasting impression against the larger capacity cars on the Tarmac at Windsor Field. (David Ash Archive, courtesy Michael Eaton)

Don Forbes lived in Rockland County, New York but obviously had an affinity with the southern part of America, as witnessed by his car bearing the Confederate flag. His was a standard production XK120, not quite in the same league as the M specification Jaguars that attended Nassau in 1954. (David Ash Archive, courtesy Michael Eaton)

Duncan Black had finished in 4th place in Class FM of the SCCA National Championship in 1954 and decided to try his luck at Nassau with the Lester-MG. He was not disappointed as he finished 5th in the Nassau Trophy Race, though it irked him that John Von Neumann, driving a Porsche, had beaten him to win Class FM.
(David Ash Archive, courtesy Michael Eaton)

as I can tell, were only open to residents of the Bahamas. Three main car races took place, the Resident's Race won by Juan Fernandez driving an Austin-Healey 100, the Bahamas Automobile Cup won by Alfonso De Portago in a Ferrari, and the Nassau Trophy Race won by Masten Gregory, also driving a Ferrari.

Alfonso De Portago was, to say the least, a colourful character. Renowned internationally for both his driving skills and his taste in beautiful women, he came to Nassau with the Ferrari 750 Monza. Just as Goldschmidt's car had entered the Carrera Panamericana, similarly the Monza had also been entered. A blown engine put it out of the race in Mexico, but hard work by a pair of mechanics got it back in working order for the Bahamas races. Portago gave thanks for their efforts by winning the Bahamas Automobile Cup and finishing second to Masten Gregory in the Nassau Trophy Race. (R Rose, Terry O'Neil Collection)

1955
Consolidation

The Speed Weeks organisers considered their efforts of 1954 successful and, as a result, were encouraged to be more pro-active in their approach to the 1955 event by widely advertising the races. Maybe a little too pro-active, as a flood of 200 applications arrived for the 100 places available. Having accepted the 100 applications of their choosing it gave the organisers the scope to vary and increase the number of races, and accordingly, a Ferrari Race was introduced into the event. Interestingly, the 100 figure turned out to be somewhat arbitrary, as some drivers brought several cars with them while some cars ended up with several drivers for different races. Such was the wondrous complexity of this relaxed event.

NASSAU TROPHY ROAD RACES
WINDSOR FIELD ROAD COURSE

Official PICTORIAL 2/-

Bahamas Automobile Club
December 5 through 11 1955

1955 programme cover.
(Terry O'Neil Collection)

Sir Sydney Oakes and guest Donald Healey survey the scene at Windsor Field. As well as entering a couple of cars for the races, Donald Healey also donated a cup for the event, namely The Donald Healey Sportsmanship Award.
(Felicity Oakes-Simpson. Terry O'Neil Collection)

Austin-Healey team driver Lance Maklin (left) lines up with Hollywood film actor Jackie Cooper, Roy Jackson-Moore, who was also a team driver, Stirling Moss, Lady Greta Oakes, Donald Healey and Sir Sydney Oakes at Windsor Field.

George Waltman brought this rare Fiat engined Special to Nassau. His small car was very slow and considered a danger, so George agreed to run the first lap of the Nassau Trophy Race, pit for the duration of the race, then come out again for the final lap so as to classify as a finisher.
(George Waltman. Terry O'Neil Collection)

Look in the programme for the race entrants and you will find Lyle Lee driving car #62. 'Lyle Lee' was in fact Jan Brundage. Having just taken on a Volkswagen franchise in Miami, Jan thought it prudent to adopt a different name for the purposes of driving a Porsche at Nassau. Unfortunately for him it appears that he was too intent on driving to bother counting the laps covered in the Porsche Race, stopping after 4 of the scheduled 5, thinking he had won the race.
(Courtesy Jan Brundage)

The social aspects of the event were planned as carefully as the races by the organisers. A welcoming party for drivers and crews ensured everyone was at ease and, with a different party to go to on each night of the Speed Weeks, there was plenty to look forward to, irrespective of how things were working out on the track.

The motorcycle races were eliminated from the programme because of insurance difficulties, but extra car events were introduced, such as the Formula Three Race, the Ferrari Race, the Porsche Race and the Jaguar Race. The Governor's Trophy Race replaced the Bahamas Automobile Cup and was won by Alfonso De Portago in a Ferrari, while the Nassau Trophy Race was won by Phil Hill in yet another Ferrari.

Novice driver Louis Kenedy entered his Jaguar XK120 in the Resident's Race, finishing 3rd overall behind the Jaguars of David Albury and 'Red' Crise, the latter considering himself an honorary resident for the purpose of this race.
(Courtesy Patsy Kenedy Bolling Archive)

Alfonso De Portago was both popular and successful as a driver. His success at Nassau can be measured by the impressive array of silverware he collected during the event.
(Bahamas News Agency. Terry O'Neil Collection)

1956
Final races at
Windsor Field

After two successful years the Speed Weeks event was now a permanent fixture on the race calendar and, for the 1956 races, 120 invitations were sent out and just as quickly returned by the lucky recipients. It was not just the event organisers who were doing well, as official figures showed that tourism to Nassau had increased by 65 per cent in early December compared to the same period before the Speed Weeks took place.

Alfonso De Portago had brought with him the Ferrari 860 Monza that he had driven to 3rd place in the race at Caracus. It proved quick and reliable, as reflected by his 2nd place to Shelby in the Governor's Trophy Race and 3rd place in the Nassau Trophy Race.
(Bahamas News Agency. Terry O'Neil Collection)

1956 programme cover.
(Terry O'Neil Collection)

The standard of competition was improving year by year, with the likes of Carroll Shelby, Phil Hill, Stirling Moss, Masten Gregory, and Alfonso De Portago among many other talented drivers vying for the many trophies on offer. They brought with them some of the newest competition cars as the manufacturers recognised the publicity value of winning one of the major trophies at Nassau. Significantly, and for the first time, a factory team of cars turned up. Chevrolet decided to send a team of three Corvettes to Nassau but entered the cars, as a matter of convenience, through Linsey Hopkins, a major shareholder of Coca-Cola.

Some resurfacing work had been carried out at Windsor Field during the year: as the track was so infrequently used, sand had been spread over the track by the wind, making the surface akin to a skating rink. Before practice for the racing could commence, a rotary broom was produced to help clear the track – after a fashion.

The Le Mans line-up for the Nassau Trophy included an official entry of three cars from Chevrolet. The three Corvettes were entered under the name of Ed Cole through Linsey Hopkins, a major shareholder of Coca-Cola. Each car had been race prepared by the Chevrolet Engineering Centre with a specially tuned engine and a Ramjet fuel injection system installed. (Courtesy Joe Trybulec)

De Portago's Ferrari 860 Monza suffered damage in a collision with an Austin-Healey 100. Interestingly, the photo shows damage but also the numberplate on De Portago's car which plainly shows a number 57. From a similar layout on other plates, the number would indicate the year. So, who got it wrong? (Bahamas News Agency. Terry O'Neil Collection)

The social scene for the competitors was even more frantic this year, as different hotels competed to host the celebrity parties, and the lucky guests among their number received an invitation to attend a cocktail party at Hillcrest House, hosted by Lady Oakes.

On the track, Carroll Shelby and Howard Hively won their respective sections of the Governor's Trophy Race, both driving Ferraris, but the Ferrari dominance was at last broken when Stirling Moss drove a Maserati 300S to victory in the Nassau Trophy Race.

A 'one off' innovation was made at this years event with the addition to the programme of the International Power Boat Regatta. Crise was a keen boat enthusiast and he could not resist the opportunity of adding this prestigious event to the Speed Weeks races. Held at Lake Cunningham, it took place the week after the car races.

Alfonso De Portago and Louise King in conversation. (Bahamas News Agency, Terry O'Neil Collection)

1957
A move to Oakes Field

1957 saw a major upheaval for the organisers of the Speed Weeks as the venue for the races changed. Windsor Field had been handed over to the Civil Aviation Authority because of its need to increase capacity, due to more flights arriving at Nassau, and in return, the old civil airport at Oakes Field was made available for the

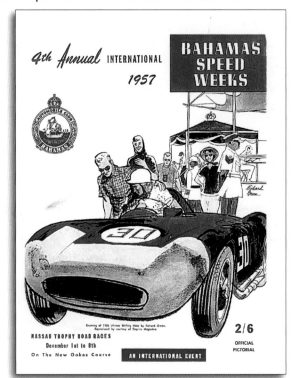

1957 programme cover. (Terry O'Neil Collection)

1957 map of Oakes Course. (Terry O'Neil Collection)

races. Despite the less than satisfactory condition of the airfield, a 5 mile anti-clockwise course was laid out over the expanse of runways, and incorporated seventeen turns, with a pit area to the inside of the track. To help carry out an initial programme of development at the site, the Island Legislature donated £50,000, which was spent on building 104 covered pit areas, a press box and a large scoreboard. A new footbridge spanning the track for the safety and convenience of the spectators had also been erected and was donated by Esso Standard Oil.

Over 200 applications to attend the races were made and, of these, 120 were accepted by the Race Committee. One name missing this year was that of Alfonso De Portago. He had been killed earlier in the year competing in the Mille Miglia race in Italy. His sad loss was reflected in the actions of the Speed Weeks organisers, as, in a mark of respect to De Portago's memory, 'Red' Crise permanently withdrew the number thirteen from cars competing at the event.

Driver Curtis Turner and entrant Jerry Earl stand in front of the Chevrolet Corvette SR2, one of two race prepared cars with a fuel-injected 283 cubic inch engine installed. Curtis Turner, who made his name in NASCAR racing, drove the car to victory in the 10-lap Memorial GT Race. (Bahamas News Agency. Terry O'Neil Collection)

Denise McCluggage was one of the most prolific lady drivers on the East Coast of America and was up against the 'Best from the West' in the form of Ruth Levy. In Heat One of the Ladies" Race the honours went to Denise, edging out Ruth by two feet on the finish line. Denise was driving a Porsche 550 while Ruth had borrowed an Aston-Martin from Stirling Moss. The second heat saw the battle re-commence, but this time Ruth tried too hard and rolled the car, leaving Denise to win the race.
(Bahamas News Agency. Terry O'Neil Collection)

A GT Race was introduced into the programme and was won by Curtis Turner, who had made his name in NASCAR racing, driving a Corvette SR2 belonging to Jerry Earl. The Nassau Tourist Trophy was won by Masten Gregory, driving a Maserati 450S, while the Governor's Trophy Race for under 2-litre cars was won by Ed Crawford in a Porsche 550 Spyder, and the over 2-litre race by Phil Hill in a Ferrari.

The fate of Stirling Moss' results all revolved around the accident involving Ruth Levy; funny how things turn out sometimes. Moss was not particularly pleased with the way the Aston was performing, but when Ruth Levy rolled the car Moss was left without a ride in the Nassau Trophy Race. A convoluted deal between Jan de Vroom, Luigi Chinetti and Temple Buell resulted in Moss sitting on the grid in a Ferrari 290MM, and as most good stories go, it had a happy ending as Moss crossed the finish line in first place. (Bahamas News Agency. Terry O'Neil Collection)

The young and talented Ricardo Rodriguez had taken the race scene by storm, and on this, his first trip to Nassau, made it a memorable occasion for his admirers. He finished second in the Governor's Trophy Race for under 2-litre cars, then finished eighth overall in the Nassau Trophy Race, gaining first in Class FM with a Porsche 550A Spyder. (Bahamas News Agency. Terry O'Neil Collection)

Ricardo Rodriguez never lost his strong family ties. The whole family would attend the races to watch Ricardo and his brother Pedro. Rodriguez Senior was the driving force behind the brothers' success and was always trying to negotiate deals to get his boys the best cars. Ricardo is pictured here with his sister, Conchita.
(Bahamas News Agency. Terry O'Neil Collection)

David Ash had remained loyal to the MG marque and had purchased an MGA. Unfortunately his loyalty was not repaid by results as the car expired on the 6th lap of the Governor's Trophy Race, never to be seen again at the event.
(David Ash Archive, courtesy Michael Eaton)

In an unexpected turn of events, Stirling Moss won the Nassau Trophy Race driving a borrowed Ferrari. His Aston-Martin had been severely damaged by Ruth Levy in the Ladies' Race, which left Moss without a car. A convoluted deal was struck for Moss to drive the Ferrari, part of the deal being that the accelerator pedal be repositioned from a central position to a conventional configuration. Despite being unfamiliar with the car, Moss won the race by over a minute ahead of Carroll Shelby.

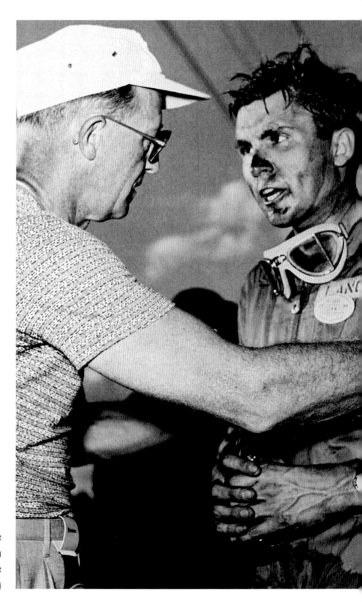

Lance Reventlow is pictured after taking part in one of the races. The Maserati 200S that he shared with Chuck Daigh under-performed against the Ferrari 500 Mondial in the main races. (Bahamas News Agency. Terry O'Neil Collection)

1958
Oakes Course; a
change of direction

1958 signalled a wind of change in the organisation of sports car racing in America – an accelerating change from amateur to professional status for drivers. This was brought about by the United States Auto Club, introducing a series of sports car races to challenge the SCCA amateur dominance in this sector of motor racing. Inevitably, the consequences of that action would spill over to the event at Nassau as some of the drivers no longer found it acceptable to race just for fun and trophies. Red Crise and the Bahamas Automobile Club now found it necessary to introduce prize money

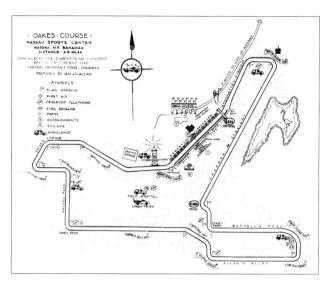

1958 new track layout. (Terry O'Neil Collection)

*1958 programme cover.
(Terry O'Neil Collection)*

for the races, but there was still the problem of SCCA members accepting the 'A' Class invitation that allowed free transportation and accommodation for the driver and helpers. The SCCA deemed that to be payment in kind. Eventually, the SCCA had to step down, but a compromise was worked out whereby the invited driver would pay a $150.00 fee to cover the 'A' Class invitation, or $100.00 for a 'B' Class invitation. As part of the deal, starting money would not be paid out by Crise to any of the drivers. A number of the 'professional' drivers were upset by this decision and Moss, Bonnier, Gendebien, Hugus, Erickson and Gregory all boycotted the event. It was reported that Moss had asked for $2000 starting money, but Crise refused to pay it. "The Bahamas Automobile Club cannot, and will not, pay starting money. We don't need the name drivers, I would rather field 100 second-rate cars than 18 or 20 first-rate cars."

Many of the cars arrived at Nassau harbour aboard the SS Florida. Typical of so many of the private entries, Ray Heppenstall transported both personal and race equipment in the car, something that could prove to be a logistical nightmare for the owners of small cars. Ray entered the DB Panhard in the Nassau Tourist Trophy Qualifying Race placing 11th, but failed to complete one lap in the actual race. Three days later he was back to win Class GM in the Nassau Memorial Race. (Charles Stockey. Alexis Callier Collection)

On the two occasions when they met head-to-head driving similar D B Panhards, Howard Hanna had the edge on Ray Heppenstall, finishing one place above him both times. (Courtesy Tim Hendley)

Ferraris were well represented at Nassau. Ed Martin in his 250TR leads the 250TR driven by Pedro Rodriguez. In the Nassau Trophy Race Rodriguez finished second to the Scarab of Reventlow and Daigh, while Ed Martin finished in third place. (Courtesy Tim Hendley)

While Pedro was driving the Ferrari 250TR, younger brother Ricardo was in the Porsche 550A Spyder, and acquitted himself well in the Governor's Trophy Race by finishing first in Class F and fifth overall. He was not so fortunate in the Nassau Trophy Race, dropping out on lap 17. (Courtesy Tim Hendley)

The pair of Scarabs at the start of the Nassau Trophy Race. Reventlow jumps in car #37 while Daigh settles in car #97. Daigh's Scarab let him down on the 3rd lap of the race, but Reventlow generously let him share the driving duties in his car. Between the pair of them they drove the car to victory, giving the Scarab a unique 'double' as Reventlow had already won the Governor's Trophy Race in that car.
(Charles Stockey. Alexis Callier Collection)

A picture of power and beauty. Ed Crawford's well presented Maserati 450S turned heads, both for its looks and for its performance, as Ed finished 3rd in the Governor's Trophy Race and 4th in the Nassau Trophy Race with this car.
(Charles Stockey. Alexis Callier Collection)

Lady Greta Oakes relaxes in the pit lane with a cigarette and cup of coffee. Health and safety…forget it!
(Charles Stockey. Alexis Callier Collection)

The Nisonger Sadler Team brought two cars down from Canada for the event – and possibly wished it had not bothered. Dogged by bad luck, its members failed to finish a race between them. Car #2 is receiving attention after running over a marker light and damaging the rear half-shaft. At the time, Bob Said was at the wheel of the car.
(Charles Stockey. Alexis Callier Collection)

Denise McCluggage borrowed Jim Lowe's Lotus XI for the Ladies" Race. In Heat One she encountered gearbox troubles and retired the car, but went on to win the second heat in the same car after repairs were carried out.
(Charles Stockey. Alexis Callier Collection)

Following a few near misses on the pit apron in 1957, the race committee decided to make sweeping changes to Oakes Course. The track race direction was changed from anti-clockwise to clockwise, the long straightway had been narrowed to 50 feet in width, and a portion of the track excluded to make the circuit shorter. This new layout measured 4.5 miles in distance.

There was a perceptible change towards the use of big-bore American engines this year. Chevrolet-powered Scarabs, a Pontiac-powered Maserati, a Sadler, a Chevrolet Special and a Ferrari-Corvette added a new dimension to the line-up of cars.

The weather was not in favour of the organisers, driving rain causing several races to be delayed and re-scheduled for later in the week, which resulted in the organisation being stretched to capacity.

When the races eventually got under way, Jim Jeffords, driving a Corvette SR2, won the Nassau Tourist Trophy Race. Lance Reventlow won the Governor's Trophy Race and also co-drove the winning Scarab with Chuck Daigh to win the Nassau Trophy Race. Italian car domination of the races had at last been well and truly broken.

Nearly ready for the off. The start of the 5-lap Nassau Tourist Trophy Race with the Fiat Abarth of K. Moore on the front row. He failed to finish due to mechanical problems, but managed to fix the car in time for the Tourist Trophy 25-lap race, finishing 3rd in Class G, having been moved from Class H. (Charles Stockey. Alexis Callier Collection)

Oliver Schmidt's Mitchell Special appeared to spend more time in the pits than on the track, judging by the array of tools on display. When it eventually came out for the Nassau Trophy Race the car managed just 28 laps before having to retire. (Charles Stockey. Alexis Callier Collection)

Leave me alone! At the same time as being partially protected by the family, Ricardo would learn to tolerate the attention of the photographers and the press as he got older. (Charles Stockey. Alexis Callier Collection)

Jim Jeffords' 'Purple People Eater' (Chevrolet Corvette SR2) delighted the crowd by winning the Nassau Tourist Trophy Race. Jim appears happy to have won the trophy. He continued his run of success and also won Class B in the Nassau Memorial Trophy Race later in the week. (Charles Stockey. Alexis Callier Collection)

1959
Politics and racing

If 1958 had been difficult for the Speed Weeks organisers in dealing with professionalism, 1959 would bring a new challenge, not from the competitors but, from the politicians in the Bahamas. Starting money would be paid this year, and a package of some $96,000 had been set aside by the organisers to pay for transport, accommodation, and cash prizes, a large portion of that total coming from the Bahamas Development Board. This lavish commitment made the Bahamas Speed Weeks the top paying sports car event in the world, and Crise hoped to entice more European drivers to the races.

In political terms, the Development Board's decision to commit the money had caused a deep division between the political parties. The opposition party in the Bahamas, the Progressive Liberal Party, had been raising questions as to the benefits accruing from the Speed Weeks, and objected to the large sums of money being spent on the event. The point was made that "The large prize money awarded to the drivers could more wisely be spent if it was applied to aiding the under-privileged Bahamian people. The money could have built two schools for the local community."

While the organisers could keep their heads down for the moment, Crise did have the foresight to make sure that criticism was kept out of the foreign press by offering free accommodation to members of the press corps.

Away from the political war of words, preparations were being made for the races. A staggering 400 applications had been received by the organisers though many of them were regretfully returned. Ninety of the 'A' Class invitations were sent out together with numerous 'B' Class invitations, the latter excluded free transportation. One new feature was incorporated into the programme, the World Karting Championships, held on one small section of Oakes Course during the evening of 5th December. Whilst it proved popular with the drivers, the floodlights were inadequate and the event dragged on into the early hours of Sunday morning.

Acceptance into the Nassau Tourist Trophy Race was enforced more rigorously this year, the race being won by John Cuevas in a Porsche 356A Carrera, while the under 2-litre Governor's Trophy Race was won by Holbert in a Porsche 718RSK. The over 2-litre race went to Stirling Moss, driving an Aston-Martin DBR2, and a similar car won the Nassau Trophy, but this time in the hands of George Constantine.

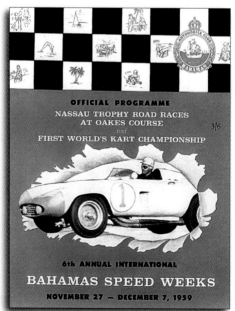

1959 programme cover.
(Terry O'Neil Collection)

All cars that entered the Speed Weeks were subject to scrutineering by members of the Bahamas Automobile Club. This process was carried out a couple of days prior to the races. The Aston-Martin DB4 GT to be driven by Stirling Moss arrived in Nassau with its previous race number still displayed on the car. The Porsche 356A Carrera was driven by Jonny Cuevas and won the Nassau Tourist Trophy Race. (Courtesy Lee Hoffman)

The front row line-up for the Nassau Tourist Trophy 5-lap race. Number 89, Smolen's Austin-Healey 3000, stands next to the Aston-Martin DB2 with a Jaguar engine installed. (Courtesy Tim Hendley)

John Collins from Texas brought his AC Bristol to Nassau, more in hope than expectation, and entered four races. Credit to the car and driver, they finished each of the races, the best result coming in the Nassau Memorial Trophy Race, where the car finished 4th overall and 2nd in Class E. (J Mauro. Terry O'Neil Collection)

The Governor's Trophy Race for under 2-litre cars proved a close race for Roy Schechter, Harry Blanchard and Pedro Rodriguez. Rodriguez, in a Dino 196S, finished in second position behind Holbert, while Blanchard was third and Schechter fifth, both driving Porsche 718 RSK models. (Courtesy Tim Hendley)

Nassau resident and airline pilot Hans Schenk made time to race his Austin-Healey 3000 in the Residents' Race. Unfortunately, he could do no better than finish in 20th place. (J Mauro. Terry O'Neil Collection)

Tim Mayer borrowed Smolen's Austin-Healey 3000 to drive in the Austin-Healey Race. He started well and managed to keep ahead of the other nine competitors to win the race. Tom Boorman in an Austin-Healey 100 finished in second place. (Courtesy Ferret Fotographics)

The Aston Martin DB2-Jaguar driven by H Brown is about to be passed by the Aston-Martin DBR2, driven by Stirling Moss in the Governor's Trophy over 2-litre Race. Moss went on to win the race ahead of the Maserati T61, owned and driven by Gus Andrey, whereas Brown had to retire his Aston-Martin after encountering mechanical troubles. (Courtesy Tim Hendley)

The futuristic-looking General Motors experimental Chevrolet Stingray SR2 did not perform to expectations. The car failed to finish in the Governor's Trophy Race, though it did finish in eleventh place in the Nassau Trophy Race with Dick Thompson behind the wheel. (Courtesy Tim Hendley)

Gaston Andrey was given the opportunity of driving Mike Garber's Maserati T61, finishing second to Stirling Moss in the over 2-litre Governor's Trophy Race and seventh in the Nassau Trophy Race, albeit not running at the end due to being involved in an accident which caused the car to ignite. Luckily, the flames were quickly doused and not too much damage resulted. (Courtesy Ferret Fotograhics)

The Maserati 450S #98 was entered at Nassau by Jim Hall, who bought the car from Temple Buell. Carroll Shelby was nominated to drive the car and, in the Governor's Trophy 5-lap Heat, finished in 3rd place. Shelby decided to drive a Maserati T61 in the Nassau Trophy, which was to prove fortunate for Lloyd Ruby as it left the 450S vacant. Ruby, in another 450S #4509, experienced trouble at the start of the Nassau Trophy Race, so dived into the pits and exchanged his car for the vacant 450S #4508. Ruby finished 15th overall after a delayed start. Mechanic 'Red' Byron is pictured in the car prior to Shelby using it in the Governor's Trophy Race. (Courtesy Ferret Fotographics)

Art Habersin entered his Austin-Healey 3000 at Nassau and had a busy week, finishing 14th in the Nassau Tourist Trophy, 13th in the Governor's Trophy, 4th in the Austin-Healey Race and 12th in the Nassau Memorial Race.
(J Mauro. Terry O'Neil Collection)

Sir Sydney Oakes drove his Alfa Romeo Giulietta Spyder in the Residents' Race, finishing in 8th place out of a field of 18 starters. (J Mauro. Terry O'Neil Collection)

David Albury was a resident of Nassau and joined in the spirit of things with an uncompetitive Austin-Healey Sprite. He failed to finish in both the Austin-Healey Race and the Residents' Race. (J Mauro. Terry O'Neil Collection)

Heather Bethell was a resident of the Bahamas and the Bethell family were close friends of author Leslie Charteris. Heather decided to place her own version of The Saint on her Austin-Healey Sprite. Pitted against far more experienced drivers she finished 5th in the Ladies' Race and 10th in the Residents' Race. (J Mauro. Terry O'Neil Collection)

1960
Single seat racing, Formula Junior

Several changes to the make-up of the schedule of events heralded commencement of the 1960 Speed Weeks at Nassau. Kart racing had been introduced in 1959 as an evening event, but this year was more prominently featured as two full days' activity, including World Championship Races prior to the sports car racing. Also new this year was the introduction of Formula Junior racing, bringing single seat racing to Nassau for the first time. Formula Junior was a growth sector of the racing scene in America and, by successfully negotiating for the races to take place at Nassau, Red Crise was able to hold the final round of the Pan-American Championship series there, as part of the Speed Weeks event.

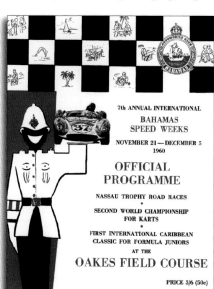

1960 programme cover.
(Terry O'Neil Collection)

Action from the Class A/B Stock Kart Race held on 25th November. Jack Saunders in/on an Xterminator leads an assortment of Karts around the half-mile long track. This particular race was won by Carlos Peruneda driving a Go Kart. (Courtesy Ferret Fotographics)

It wasn't just the adults that had fun at Nassau. There was a special Kart Class for Juniors. (I think they meant infants!) I don't know the name of the child driving this Kart, but they sure started them young. (Courtesy Ferret Fotographics)

The introduction of Formula Junior cars brought a new dimension to the racing at Nassau. Two 5-lap heats were run prior to the 12-lap final, the Pan-American Race. Twenty cars lined up for the final, among them #23, the Cooper T52-BMC driven by Humphries. He finished third in his heat and seventh in the final. (Courtesy Ferret Fotographics)

The Le Mans-style start to the 252 mile Nassau Trophy Race. 44 cars started the race with an Austin-Healey, four Ferraris and a Sadler Mk II making a quick getaway. Last from the line was Stirling Moss in the Lotus XIX, having stalled the car. After a push-start he sped down the pit straight and into Crise's Corner, where an A-frame collapsed and the front end of the car hit the road. Exit Stirling Moss from the race. As one commentator put it "about 50 cents a foot for as far as the Lotus went," referring to the $5000 appearance money that Moss picked up. (Bahamas News Agency. Terry O'Neil Collection)

Peter Jackson ran his Austin-Healey Sprite in the Nassau Tourist Trophy Race, and came away with a Class G victory. (Courtesy Ferret Fotographics)

Moss enjoyed far better luck in the Nassau Tourist Trophy Race. Driving Rob Walker's dark blue Ferrari 250GT SWB, he finished first ahead of three other Ferraris with an effortless display of driving. (Courtesy Ferret Fotographics)

The timetable for the Speed Weeks was becoming elongated, and many of the competitors could not be bothered to stay for the full period despite the lure of the parties. In truth, even they had changed; too many hangers-on were there just to be seen, and the drivers spent only a short period of time in their company before moving on to more intimate clubs and restaurants. The driving was also becoming more intense due to the prizes on offer. The day of the 'gentleman driver' was gone, replaced by a more brash set of people whose attitude caused a certain amount of resentment with the local populace in general and hoteliers in particular.

Ricardo Rodriguez guides the Ferrari 250 TR59 around Oakes Course on the way to second place in the Nassau Trophy Race. He shared the car with his brother Pedro, as Pedro's own 250 TR59 had received substantial damage in an accident in the Governor's Trophy Race. (Courtesy Tim Hendley)

Dan Gurney drives his Lotus XIX to victory in the Nassau Trophy Race. This was the first of three victories the Lotus XIX would achieve at the Speed Weeks.
(Courtesy Tim Hendley)

The other aspect of the event that had changed was the influence of commercial coverage of the races. CBS-TV was on hand and insisted that the scheduling of certain races be changed for its convenience. Ironically, the weather usually had the last say and things revolved around that, not the TV company.

The Nassau Tourist Trophy had a familiar name added to the Cup, that of Stirling Moss, who won the event in a Ferrari 250SWB. Ferrari was back to winning ways. The Italian marque also won the Governor's Trophy Race when Ricardo Rodriguez drove his Ferrari 250TR to victory, and narrowly missed out on a clean sweep of the major trophies when coming second in the Nassau Trophy Race, behind Dan Gurney's Lotus XIX.

1961
Two for Dan Gurney

Additional help for the race organisers was at hand for the 1961 Speed Weeks. A motorclub had been formed on the island of New Providence, the Bahamas Racing and Sports Car Club. From the body of the membership, volunteers, albeit with limited experience, stepped forward to perform flag marshalling and time-keeping duties. These volunteers were in addition to those who already flew in from Miami to help with the races.

For the third year in succession, karts were featured at Nassau, and Formula Junior cars also returned. In addition to the karts, 32 drivers came from Detroit with Midget Racers to compete in the final rounds of the All World Championship. It was also noticeable that more team owners were arriving in Nassau. For this year's event, Rosebud Racing Team turned up with a large semi-trailer full of cars,

Disembarkation at Nassau harbour was a tricky job and fairly labour-intensive. From the boat the cars were driven to Oakes Course for scrutineering before the races.
(John Owen. Terry O'Neil Collection)

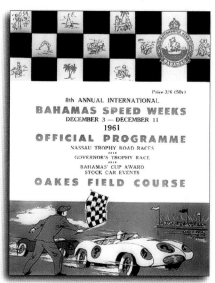

1961 programme cover.
(Terry O'Neil Collection)

Team Roosevelt had three cars, Scuderia Serenissima turned up with a Maserati T63 and a Ferrari 250TRI/61, and the North American Racing Team entered three cars. With competitive cars becoming more expensive, privateers were finding it difficult to match the teams on an equal basis, so more drivers were offering their services to the teams instead. The 'amateur' privateers were realistic as they came for the fun and were hopeful of picking up a Class win in some of the races. If money came their way, then that was a bonus.

Despite spending money on improving the track surface, it was still pretty bumpy, and the organisers received a number of complaints as the cars began losing bits and pieces as they lapped. Stirling Moss did a repeat performance of 1960 and won the Nassau Tourist Trophy in a Ferrari 250SWB, and Pedro Rodriguez emulated his brother's feat of 1960 by winning the Governor's Trophy Race. The Formula Junior Pan-American Championship Race went to Pete Lovely, while Dan Gurney proved that last year's victory in the Lotus XIX was no fluke by winning the Nassau Trophy Race again this year in the same car.

Guido Lollobrigida's Maserati 300S arrives at Nassau docks. The car was entered by the Miami based Sorocaima Racing Team, but only appeared in the Nassau Trophy Race where it lasted for 17 laps before retiring. For those who are wondering, Guido was supposedly a cousin of Gina. (Flip Schulke, Courtesy Willem Oosthoek Collection)

Red mist descends as the Residents' Race takes place. #N8 finds that adhesion is not that great in an Austin-Healey Sprite. (Courtesy Tim Hendley)

Formula Junior racing had taken off in America and the number of entries in the event in Nassau reflected that fact. 25 cars started the Pan-American Championship Race. The race was won by Pete Lovely driving a Lotus XX ahead of Pat Pigott in a similar car, Roger Penske in a Cooper T56 and Mark Donohue driving an Elva 300. (John Owen. Terry O'Neil Collection)

Nassau resident Patsy Kenedy entered her Jaguar XK120 in the Residents' Race and was going nicely when ...
(Courtesy Patsy Kenedy Bolling Archive)

Milling around the pit lane prior to the start of the Nassau Trophy Race. Cars were lined up by engine capacity size, largest at the top of the line-up. The group of Lotus cars was about half-way along the line. (Courtesy Roy Schechter Collection)

... the car caught fire. Luckily, Patsy escaped the inferno but could do nothing about her car. The trouble started when the battery cable shorted on the car.
(Courtesy Patsy Kenedy Bolling Archive)

Another view of the pit lane prior to the start of the Nassau Trophy Race, where Schechter's Lotus XIX stands next to the Ferrari Dino 246S of John Fulp. Car #7 is a similar Ferrari driven by Ricardo Rodriguez. So who's who in the zoo? Top left is Hap Sharp swinging helmet and goggles, and next to him event organiser Sherman 'Red' Crise wearing the Captain's hat. Top middle is Bob Schroeder and upper middle is Roy Schechter with his back to the camera.
(Courtesy Roy Schechter Collection)

The start of the Nassau Trophy Race. Dan Gurney's Lotus, shown on the left of the photograph, is already up-to-speed while other competitors struggle to get off the line. Nino Vaccarella appears to have left a good deal of his rear tyres behind as he gets away in the Maserati T63. (Courtesy Alexis Callier Collection)

All aboard for the Nassau Trophy Race! Some drivers hated the Le Mans-style starts while others literally took it in their stride. Stirling Moss was always quick across the Tarmac (though not always so quick off the line). Next to him, also driving Lotus XIXs, are Jack Nethercutt who only survived for three laps of the race, and Dan Gurney who went on to win the race. (Courtesy Roy Schechter Collection)

Alan Connell turned up at Nassau with an interesting hybrid car, a Maserati T61 with a Ferrari 3-litre engine installed. He drove it to great effect, finishing 3rd in the Nassau Trophy Race. (Courtesy Roy Schechter Collection)

Roy Schechter made a slow start to the Nassau Trophy Race driving his Lotus XIX, and was to manage only three laps before having to retire the car, proving that not all Lotus XIXs were winners. The engine was great but the gearbox suffered from ring-and-pinion gear failure. (Courtesy Roy Schechter Collection)

Patsy Kenedy receiving a prize from the Island Governor at the Gala Dinner, held at the end of the Speed Weeks.
(Courtesy Patsy Kenedy Bolling)

1962
Lotus XIX
stranglehold

In 1962 the Speed Weeks played host to a number of new (to this part of the world) cars. Carroll Shelby brought two of his Cobras for Pabst and Krause to drive, Ford had put together a competitive package comprising of a Falcon and a Galaxie and Ferrari had introduced the 250GTO model. The 250GTO had taken the European circuits by storm and NART had raced them at Sebring and Bridgehampton with success. Avid Ferrari drivers were keen to take delivery of them, as alternative Ferrari sports prototypes were scarce and therefore expensive to purchase and to run.

On a sadder note, there was no representative of the Rodriguez family in attendance this year. Tragically, Ricardo was

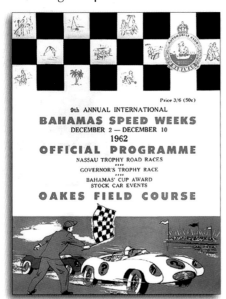

1962 programme cover.
(Terry O'Neil Collection)

killed in Mexico and Pedro had taken the decision not to attend Nassau despite being offered a 250GTO to drive by Luigi Chinetti. Maybe the reason why he turned down the offer was because it was the car that he and Ricardo had shared in their victory at Montlhéry in France.

Arch James was the official race starter at the Speed Weeks. A colourful, well-liked and respected character, he managed to keep the drivers under control. His race coats were as varied in design as any in America. Here, he wears the striped one, which replaced the plain red one, at the request of the drivers as, at speed, the drivers mistook his red coat for a red flag! (John Owen. Terry O'Neil Collection)

The organisers made a couple more changes to the event this year. Gone were the Karts and Midgets, and in came the Prototype cars to race alongside the GT and Sports cars, but only on the basis that the Prototype car weighed within 5 per cent of the original figure submitted to the FIA for other races in America and Europe. It was made known to those drivers of Prototype cars that no prize money would be coming their way, even if they won their respective race.

Another new structure also appeared at Oakes Course. A special press box was installed at the Esso bend, one of the most action-filled curves on the course. The facility was in addition to the clubhouse press box and was the structure formerly located in the vicinity of the smaller temporary Kart track.

In spite of complaints in 1961 about the condition of the track, the dented cars and, in some cases, the dented bank balance, the attractions of Nassau far outweighed the reasons not to be there and, yet again, the entry list was over-subscribed.

Had this Alfa Romeo Giulietta SZ not been photographed at the docks in Nassau, the car would have been unnoticed. It failed to make the Nassau Tourist Trophy Race, but appeared for the preliminary heat of the Governor's Trophy Race, failing after about 20 laps and did not appear again for the duration of the event.
(John Owen. Terry O'Neil Collection)

Not too many OSCA 1600 GTs made their way to America, but this particular one was sponsored by NART and raced at Nassau by Tom Fleming. Its appearance was less than memorable; failing to finish in the Nassau Tourist Trophy Race, placed a distant 35th in the Governor's Trophy Race, and failing again in the Nassau Trophy Race.
(John Owen. Terry O'Neil Collection)

Hardly a fair contest between the Ferrari 250GTO and the DB Panhard, but both drivers strove for honours. Bandini took the Ferrari to 2nd place overall in the Nassau Tourist Trophy Race, while Hagan managed 2nd in Class 1/5 GTs.
(John Owen. Terry O'Neil Collection)

The Ford Galaxie proved a handful for Dieringer but, with persistence and skill, he managed to keep the beast of a car on the track long enough to finish in 23rd place in the Nassau Tourist Trophy Race. It had plenty of speed but stopping power was a real problem. The car performed exceptionally well in the Nassau Trophy Race where Dieringer finished in 7th place. (John Owen. Terry O'Neil Collection)

Trust in thy neighbour! From the start of the Nassau Trophy Race, the crowded field approached Turn 1 under the Esso Bridge. It appears to have turned out well as everyone managed to get round this particular bend without damage. The leaders have scurried out of sight, with the mid-field cars vying for position as they go under the bridge. (Bahamas News Agency. Terry O'Neil Collection)

A mystery car turned up at Nassau for the races. I have failed to identify the car which sits on the dock-side, sporting an old race number 91. Unfortunately the badge on the car is unclear, as is the identity of the owner standing to the rear. (John Owen. Terry O'Neil Collection)

The DB Panhard belonging to Howard Hanna is unloaded from the SS Yarmouth at Nassau docks. Hanna drove this car to a Class win in the Nassau Tourist Trophy Race and the Governor's Trophy Race, though failed to finish in the Nassau Trophy Race. (John Owen. Terry O'Neil Collection)

Charlie Hayes took over the driving of the Scuderia Bear-entered Ferrari 250 GTO from Lorenzo Bandini for the Governor's Trophy Race and the Nassau Trophy Race. He finished 3rd in the Governor's Trophy Race and 5th in the Nassau Trophy Race, where the driving was shared by Ed Hugus. (John Owen. Terry O'Neil Collection)

The Ferrari 250GT SWB of Alan Wylie and the Lola OSCA of Bates and Thomas seek shelter from the heat of the sun prior to the races. The pits at Nassau offered the bare minimum when it came to contestant facilities. (John Owen. Terry O'Neil Collection)

'Local girl come good:' Patsy Kenedy came 3rd in the Residents' Race driving her Porsche 356A Carrera GT, 3rd in the Ladies' Race behind Alice Stevens and Smokey Drolet, and 6th in the 10-lap Bahamas Cup Race. Three Cooper Monaco models are lined up behind the Porsche in the hanger awaiting attention. (Courtesy Patsy Kenedy Bolling Archive)

The Pan-American Championship Race brought together the top Formula Junior drivers in America. Only six cars finished the 12-lap race, a lone Cooper T59 interloping in a bevy of Lotus finishers. Nethercutt led the race from the start and finished ahead of Dibley and Revson. (Bahamas News Agency. Terry O'Neil Collection)

Lloyd Ruby's Lotus XIX had seen better days after spinning off the course in the rain early in the Nassau Trophy Race. He called in at the pits to have the damaged bodywork removed and returned to the race. He worked his way up to second position, despite the rain pouring through the re-arranged bodywork on the car, before having to retire on the 49th lap of the race due to dropping oil pressure. (John Owen. Terry O'Neil Collection)

Glamour and yet
more glamour.
Lady Greta Oakes
standing with
Patsy Kenedy,
holding a prize at
the ball held at the
end of the Speed
Weeks. (Courtesy
Patsy Kenedy
Bolling Archive)

The Nassau Tourist Trophy preliminary race was
split into two sections: under and over 2-litres. Chuck
Cassell, driving a Porsche Abarth 356B Carrera, won
the under 2-litre section, and those waiting for the new
Ferrari 250GTOs to falter were sorely disappointed
as they claimed the first four places in the over 2-litre
race, Roger Penske taking first place. The Ferraris
repeated their performance in the 25-lap race, Penske
again taking top spot. A new name was to appear on
the Governor's Trophy, that of Hap Sharp who drove his
Cooper Monaco to victory, and likewise on the Nassau
Trophy, when Innes Ireland drove a Lotus XIX to victory,
the third time the Lotus XIX had won the race.

George Reed
turned up at
Nassau with his
Ferrari 250TR 59
but the car sat
there until the
very last race, the
Nassau Trophy.
After a promising
start it finished
in 10th place; not
bad for what was
then an old car
up against more
modern technology.
(John Owen. Terry
O'Neil Collection)

1963
American muscle

After the attempt in 1962 of the American manufacturers to be competitive against the European cars at the Speed Weeks, it was not surprising to see them return again in 1963 in a more determined mood. However, not only were they competing against the Europeans, this year they were vying against each other for dominance. In the months leading up to the Nassau races, the Ford Cobra had been successful in the races held in America, whereas the Chevrolet Corvette Grand Sport models had not fared so well. Determined to fight back, Chevrolet had replaced the standard 327ci engine with a 377ci engine and had farmed the cars out to John Mecom in Texas to race under his banner. As well as the three Grand Sport

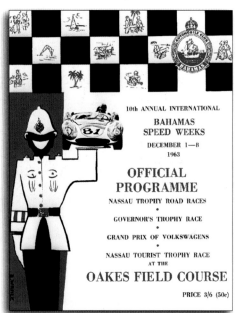

1963 programme cover.
(Terry O'Neil Collection)

One of the three Chevrolet Grand Sport models entered on behalf of the Chevrolet factory, #65 being driven by various members of the Mecom Team throughout the duration of the Speed Weeks event. (John Owen. Terry O'Neil Collection)

Maybe not the smartest rig on the island, but it did its job. Mike Gammino transported his Ferrari 250GTO to Nassau on the TMT trailer ferry San Juan then continued with the car by trailer to Oakes Course. He entered the car in the Nassau Tourist Trophy Race, finishing second, but collected the top cash prize as Augie Pabst - who came first in a Lola Mk VI GT Chevrolet - was in the prototype class and ineligible for cash prizes. (John Owen. Terry O'Neil Collection)

models, the Mecom Team also brought with it four other cars with Chevrolet engines installed. Not only did John Mecom have the cars, he also hired the services of a group of experienced sports car drivers, including Jim Hall, Augie Pabst, Dick Thompson and Roger Penske. Undoubtedly, General Motors was paying John Mecom for them as well as running the cars. Oh, and did I mention that a group of Chevrolet engineers just happened to be taking their holidays in Nassau at the same time as the races? Against this assault, Shelby had Dan Gurney, Bob Holbert, Frank Gardener, Ray Heppenstall, John Everly, Dave McDonald and Ken Miles driving Ford-powered cars.

The Mecom Team from Texas brought a selection of cars with it to Nassau, all powered by Chevrolet engines, and it was probably no coincidence that a group of Chevrolet engineers were taking a holiday in Nassau at precisely the same time that the races were on. One of the cars was the Lola Mk VI prototype, which was entered in the 5-lap GT Race and the Nassau Tourist Trophy Race. Augie Pabst drove the car to victory in both races. (John Owen. Terry O'Neil Collection)

An impressive line-up of American muscle on the start grid for the Governor's Trophy Race. A Chaparral, a Ferrari-Ford and a Chevrolet Grand Sport are on the front row, while on the second row are two more Chevrolets.
(Bahamas News Agency. Terry O'Neil Collection)

Under the footbridge and into the first bend of the Governor's Trophy Race, three of the four leading cars were the Chevrolet Grand Sport models entered by John Mecom. The four leading cars were followed into the bend by the eventual race winner, A.J. Foyt who was driving a Scarab #77. The Grand Sport models did remarkably well, finishing in 3rd, 4th and 6th places.
(John Owen. Terry O'Neil Collection)

The European challenge appeared weak by comparison. This year the Rosebud Team failed to enter the races as Innes Ireland was recuperating from a leg injury, so was unable to defend his title as Nassau Trophy winner, while only one Ferrari 250GTO turned up, that of privateer Mike Gammino. NART entered a Ferrari 250P for Pedro Rodriguez to drive, but other than that it was difficult to see where a challenge would come from.

A new phenomenon was sweeping across the motor racing world in America in the form of Formula Vee. The Volkswagen came in two forms: the road version or the single-seat form that directly replaced Formula Junior. Much less expensive than other forms of racing, it appealed to a new breed of enthusiasts. Crise was going to make sure he was catering for that market by including the Formula in the Speed Week events.

A new form of racing was introduced at Nassau to replace the Formula Junior Races. Formula Vee and VW GTs were the more affordable option and had taken off well in America. #15 is a FV Special, driven by Tom Payne in the FV Race and Heather Myers in the Ladies' Race, where she placed 3rd. (John Owen. Terry O'Neil Collection)

Cars line up for the start of the VW GT 5-lap Race. Very few modifications were allowed but the drivers took the race seriously. The cars proved comparatively slow so the races were held over short distances to prevent the spectators becoming bored. This initial VW GT Race attracted eleven entries and was won by McDaniel, ahead of Belcher and Coleman. (John Owen. Terry O'Neil Collection)

Action from the first heat of the FV Race where Lawrence #20 and Kolb #0 lead off from the start line. Kolb went on to win the race ahead of Oliver Schmidt and Lawrence, all of them driving Formcars. (John Owen. Terry O'Neil Collection)

Red Crise, in his wisdom, decided to add Prototype Class cars to the Nassau Tourist Trophy Race, so the Chevrolet Grand Sport models lined-up for the event alongside the Lola MkVI GT. The Grand Sport cars did not fare so well and retired from the race, but the Lola, driven by Augie Pabst, won the race ahead of the only Ferrari 250GTO to attend Nassau this year.

The Governor's Trophy Race was also won by a Chevrolet engined car, the Scarab driven by A J Foyt who went on to repeat his performance, and in doing so, won the Nassau Trophy Race. This not only provided Chevrolet with a win for the three big races, it also provided John Mecom with a clean sweep of the major trophies.

Jim Hall and AJ Foyt met head-to-head in both the Governor's Trophy Race and the Nassau Trophy Race. On both occasions Foyt not only got the better of Hall's Chaparral, but went on to win the races in the Mecom-entered Scarab Chevrolet. This was the first time that the same driver won both major races in the same year. (John Owen. Terry O'Neil Collection)

The Le Mans start to the Nassau Trophy Race saw a variety of cars take off in a haze of heat and tyre smoke. While larger capacity cars were placed at the head of the grid, it did not mean that they were near the front of the field after the opening laps, as some of the drivers of smaller cars were adept at this type of race start. They would be under the bridge and round the first bend by the time some of the larger cars were fired up. Only 34 of the 60 starters managed to take the finish flag. (Bahamas News Agency. Terry O'Neil Collection)

The Howe Sound Cooper Monaco Ford needed a little encouragement to re-start after a pit stop, but the combination of Heppenstall and Holbert coaxed the car to an eventual 9th position at the end of the Nassau Trophy Race. (John Owen. Terry O'Neil Collection)

After driving for up to 252 miles, Arch James holding the finish flag was a welcome sight for drivers of the Nassau Trophy Race. Gardener finished the race in 7th place in his Shelby Cobra. (Bahamas News Agency. Terry O'Neil Collection)

1964
Penske's year

The events of 1964 saw 160 interested drivers turn up to take part in an eclectic group of races. Earlier in the year, it had been mooted that a new track could be in the offing but nothing came of the rumours. Instead, the Development Board was encouraged by Crise to pump more money into Oakes Course, supposedly improving the track surface. It did this, though with a certain amount of reluctance, for fear of being sucked into a position where it would have to justify its expenditure to the public.

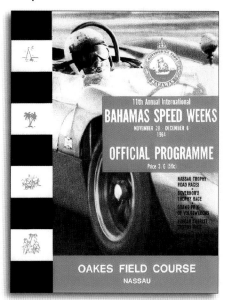

1964 programme cover.
(Terry O'Neil Collection)

Red Crise was 'talking up' the event this year, billing it as the biggest Speed Weeks yet. "We have a fabulous field of entries – far better than in any other year. These races are going to be the greatest in the world." (Quote from the *Nassau Guardian* newspaper.) Crise was well aware that circumstances outside his control were beginning to have an affect on the Speed Weeks, and his show of bravado was necessary to entice the top named drivers to Nassau again.

It looks chaotic but the system worked well for the race entrants. Their cars were housed and worked on in the large aircraft hanger that adjoined the airstrip at Oakes Course. The car in the foreground is the Ferrari 250LM belonging to Bob Grossman, next to the Brabham BT-8 of Theo Hitchcock #21. (John Owen. Terry O'Neil Collection)

Although most of the mechanical work was carried out in the hangers at Oakes Course, it was not unusual for teams to strip down their cars in the pits. Here is the Mecom Team working on the Hussein Dodge driven by AJ Foyt. (Eric della Faille. Alexis Callier Collection)

The first lap of the over 2-litre GT Race was closely contested. Ken Miles in the Shelby Cobra has a slight advantage over Jack Saunders and Roger Penske, both driving Corvette Grand Sport models, as they approach one of the bends. Penske went on to win the 5-lap race ahead of Ken Miles and Phil Hill, who piloted a Ford GT40. (John Owen. Terry O'Neil Collection)

Autosport International brought three different Renault cars to Nassau to compete in the various races. Seen here in the hanger at Oakes Course, #83 was the Alpine Renault M63 driven to 6th place by Paul Richards in the over 2-litre GT Race, and #84 the Alpine Renault A110 driven ... 17th place by W Haenelt in the same race. (John Owen-Terry O'Neil Collection)

1964 – Penske's year

Two ends of the spectrum are parked together in the pits at Nassau. On the left the diminutive BMW belonging to Ray Heppenstall, and on the right the Ferrari 250GTO of Tom Fleming. (Jack Cattell. Courtesy Ted Cianfrani)

Nassau resident Bill Easey drove the pretty Lotus Climax in both heats of the Residents' Race, where he placed 4th overall, but had less luck in the Bahamas Cup Race where he went out on the first lap with engine problems. (John Owen. Terry O'Neil Collection)

The Corvette Grand Sport driven by Jack Saunders lines up for the start of the Governor's Trophy Race. He finished 10th overall, 1st in Class 15 GTP. (Jack Cattell. Courtesy Ted Cianfrani)

John Mecom was a great supporter of the Speed Weeks, but even by his standards he surpassed Crise's expectations by arriving in Nassau with five cars. Among them was a Hussein-Dodge Zerex Special, driven by AJ Foyt. Foyt finished 2nd in the Governor's Trophy Race but retired on lap 48 of the Nassau Trophy Race, albeit claiming 19th place on distance travelled. (John Owen. Terry O'Neil Collection)

1964 – Penske's year

Chevrolet and Ford continued their fight for dominance. The Ford contingent consisted of a number of Cobras, together with two new GT40s equipped with Ford 289 engines and especially shipped over from the Ford Advanced Vehicles unit in England. Pitted against these Cobras, and the basically untested GT40s, was a group of Corvette Grand Sport models, part of a formidable array of cars entered by John Mecom. Also in the running for honours were two Ferrari 250LMs in the Prototype Class which, although down on cubic capacity in comparison to the Fords and Chevrolets, had enough power and handling capabilities to do well.

Englishman Clive Baker brought his Austin-Healey Sprite to Nassau where it was entered in the Governor's Trophy Race and the Nassau Trophy Race. He failed to finish in the Governor's Trophy event but finished in 15th place overall in the Nassau Trophy Race, 1st in Class 6/8 Prototype. (John Owen. Terry O'Neil Collection)

Perched behind the Simca Abarth 1300 Bialbero in the Scuderia Bear pits is … you guessed it … a blow-up doll! Not too sure of the significance, but Lady Greta Oakes always wore a headscarf when she came to the races … and she was quite a doll. (Jack Cattell. Courtesy Ted Cianfrani)

Pedro Rodriguez appears to have more than a passing interest in the Mecom Team Zerex Special. In the hands of Walt Hansgen it finished 3rd in the Governor's Trophy Race, and 8th in the Nassau Trophy Race. (Jack Cattell. Courtesy Ted Cianfrani)

The McLaren-Elva driven by Bruce McLaren and the Ferrari 330P driven by Pedro Rodriguez line up for the start of the Governor's Trophy Race. Rodriguez finished 4th overall but McLaren dropped out on lap 6 of the 25-lap race. (Jack Cattell. Courtesy Ted Cianfrani)

The Ford GT40s turned out to be a big disappointment and were soon withdrawn from the races, leaving the Cobras to uphold Ford's image. In the Nassau Tourist Trophy Race, Penske, driving a Grand Sport, came first ahead of the two Ferrari LMs, the little cars proving too nimble for the larger-engined Cobras. Penske turned to a Chaparral to win the Governor's Trophy Race, and co-drove with Hap Sharp in Sharp's Chaparral to win the Nassau Trophy Race ahead of Bruce McLaren.

This was the first occasion in the history of the Speed Weeks that the same driver had taken all three major trophies, albeit helped by Sharp in the Nassau Trophy Race.

It was not a good day at the office for Paul Goldsmith in the Genie-Chevrolet, or for Skip Hudson driving the Cooper Monaco Chevrolet #94. Both drivers went out of the Governor's Trophy Race in the early stages. (Jack Cattell. Courtesy Ted Cianfrani)

It looks more like an auto jumble than a workshop but in the hanger at Oakes Course space was at a premium, and mechanics had to do the best they could with what was available. (Eric della Faille. Alexis Callier collection)

Two Ford GT40s were shipped into Nassau, one for Phil Hill, the other for Bruce McLaren to drive. High expectations soon gave way to embarrassment as both cars went out of the Nassau Tourist Trophy Race in the early stages. So bad were they, that the Ford team decided to withdraw the cars and immediately shipped them back to England, before they were sent to Carroll Shelby to prepare for racing again in 1965. (John Owen. Terry O'Neil Collection)

1965
Foreseeing the future

There was no doubting that, if nothing else, 'Red' Crise was a man of foresight.

His hyping of the 1964 Speed Weeks had served his short-term interests but he was to pay the price in 1965. Everybody had considered that the standards and quality of driving had declined in the 1964 event and, as a consequence, top drivers were turning their backs on Nassau. Added to that, those top drivers were getting to grips with new rule changes in America, planning for the start of a season that would see the GT Championship disappear and have changes made to Prototype classes. In short, they had more important things to do. Despite its success over the past two years, even the Mecom Team made the decision not to attend this year.

Crise tried to make the best of a bad job by marketing 1965 as the year of the 'Rookie Drivers.' It was a plan that was very transparent and, as a

1965 programme cover.
(Terry O'Neil Collection)

The ill-fated Essex Wire Cooper Monaco King Cobra is disgorged from the bows of the TMT Biscayne at Nassau harbour. This car failed to finish a single lap in the Texas Classic Race, and was also absent from all other races. On that basis, this photograph of the car is fairly scarce.
(John Owen. Terry O'Neil Collection)

consequence of the lack of top drivers, the attraction of the event diminished in the eyes of the paying public.

Adding to his woes was the decision of the Development Board to limit the expenditure on the Speed Weeks. Politically the heat had been turned up by the Progressive Liberal Party and, with elections on the horizon, the ruling party, the United Bahamian Party, needed to steer clear of anything controversial. As a result, any money spent on the event was: "To turn the track centre into a sports complex for the benefit of the residents of the island of New Providence."

1965 - Foreseeing the future

Scrutineering at Oakes Course took place a few days before the races begun and for some, a chance to familiarise themselves with the track and its facilities. #48 is the MGB driven by Al Ackerley to 11th place in the Nassau Tourist Trophy Race. (John Owen. Terry O'Neil Collection)

Ed Hugus enjoyed no success at Nassau with his unusual combination of a Lotus 23 with a Ferrari V6 engine installed. The car lasted for seven laps in the Governor's Trophy Race but was not seen again for the duration of the event. (Bahamas News Agency. Terry O'Neil Collection)

Peter Gregg drove the Brumos-entered Porsche 904GTS in the Nassau Tourist Trophy Race and finished in second place, behind Charlie Kolb driving the more powerful Ferrari 275GTB/C. Gregg also finished second in the Porsche Race and eleventh in the Nassau Trophy Race in the same car. (John Owen. Terry O'Neil Collection)

Bruce McLaren won the Governor's Trophy Race driving his McLaren M1-B. He is pictured here being awarded the Trophy by Sir Ralph Grey, Governor of the Bahamas, while race organiser 'Red' Crise looks on.
(Bahamas News Agency. Terry O'Neil Collection)

A variety of cars appeared in the Residents' Race. Hans Schenk turned out in his newly acquired Porsche RSK Spyder, and alongside him, on the front row of the grid, was John Gordon's Lotus Elan and Patsy Kenedy's Porsche 356B Carrera. It so happens that the three cars finished the race in that order. (Courtesy Patsy Kenedy Bolling Archive.)

The first heat of the Ladies' Race attracted a field of twelve entrants, all driving borrowed Formula Vee cars. The race was won by Smokey Drolet driving a Beach FV, ahead of Patsy Kenedy in an Autodynamics FV owned by John Cologero, and Alice Bixler in a Beach FV belonging to Chandler Lawrence. (Courtesy Patsy Kenedy Bolling Archive)

33 Formula Vee cars took to the grid for the running of the 23-lap Formula Vee Grand Prix. Sweeping through one of the bends are the cars driven by Lee Cutler (#55), Charlie Kolb (#87), Bill Tharin (#46) and Ray Caldwell (#16). The race was won by Chris Amon driving a Beach FV, followed by Bruce McLaren also driving a Beach FV. (John Owen. Terry O'Neil Collection)

A delicate operation is in progress to fine-tune the extremities of the bodywork, and it looks as if the Oldsmobile engine in the Mirage is being fine-tuned as well! (John Owen. Terry O'Neil Collection)

With a backdrop of hundreds of spectators awaiting the 252 mile Nassau Trophy Race, 57 of the 58 drivers rush to their high-powered machines in a Le Mans start. One driver was obviously excused and stands at the back of his car.

Although the car looked resplendent, the Lotus 40 failed to impress AJ Foyt. The car managed only 3 laps in the Governor's Trophy Race, and expired after 14 laps of the Nassau Trophy Race. The car was given with the dubious distinction of being "a Lotus 30 with ten more faults." (John Owen. Terry O'Neil Collection)

The McLaren Elva-Chevrolet was a big disappointment for Charlie Hayes, as it failed to finish in both the Governor's Trophy Race and the Nassau Trophy Race. (John Owen. Terry O'Neil Collection)

Tom Payne had an eventful week at Nassau after his AC Cobra suffered from fuel starvation on the last lap of the Nassau Tourist Trophy Race, which cost him the race, Tom then fell into a garage pit and injured himself. Bob Grossman took over to drive the car in the Nassau Trophy Race, where he finished 5th overall, 1st in Class 13/14 GT. (John Owen. Terry O'Neil Collection)

The one redeeming feature for Crise was that a few owners brought with them their Prototype cars that, less than nine months later, would be participating in a newly formed Can-Am series of races. These cars were allowed to compete with the sports cars in the Governor's Trophy and the Nassau Trophy Races, and it was hoped that their participation would encourage interest in the event.

The Nassau Tourist Trophy was won by Charlie Kolb, somewhat fortuitously, when Tom Payne's Cobra ran out of fuel on the last lap. Bruce McLaren won the Governor's Trophy Race in his McLaren M1B, a car that would appear in future Can-Am Races. Hap Sharp had better luck this year and won the Nassau Trophy Race in a Chaparral, this time without the aid of Roger Penske.

The remains of Jim Hall's Chaparral after he spun off the road following the collapse of the front suspension unit. To make matters worse, he slid into a Fiat that had already come off the road in the same spot, and the owner asked Hall to pay for the damage to his car.
(John Owen. Terry O'Neil Collection)

Everyone is an expert when it comes to sorting out what went wrong. But who was right? Was it the front wheel, the rear wheel or the steering wheel that caused Jim Hall's Chaparral to leave the road?
(John Owen. Terry O'Neil Collection)

1966
The final scene

1966 was to signal the last Speed Weeks event. According to Red Crise, 1966 was the 12 $^{9}/_{10}$ Speed Weeks event, and nearly all the literature reflected his wishes due to the elimination of the number 13 from the races, following the death of the holder of that number, Alfonso De Portago. Call it what you like, it still turned out to be unlucky thirteen for the organisers, as everything turned sour for them.

Red Crise hung on to the hope that, by gathering as many of the Can-Am cars together as he could from the new Can-Am series held in America and Canada, he could instil new life into the Speed Weeks. It was a forlorn hope, as many of the top names in Can-Am had packed their bags and had transported their tired machinery home after the last race in Las Vegas. The old guard from

Sometimes it was easier to drive the cars to Oakes Course from the Dock at Nassau than wait for a transporter. Road legal or not, two Formula Vee cars weave their way through the traffic having just left the dock area. #85 was the Autodynamics FV of Richard Beers and #41 the Beach FV of Larry Le Pine. (Courtesy Ferret Fotographics)

1966 programme cover. (Terry O'Neil Collection)

America and Europe also stayed away in the main, whilst the event seemed not to appeal to the young up-and-coming drivers.

A few months prior to the event, bad luck struck with the death of one of the founder members of the Speed Weeks, Sir Sydney Oakes. He was killed instantly when his car hit a lamp-post. During November, the threat of a general strike during the build-up to the Speed Weeks event threw Crise's plans into confusion.

It was averted at the last minute, but left an unstable situation.

Just to add to the organisers' woes, the Israeli-owned boat, the SS Nili that had been chartered to carry the cars to Nassau, was impounded by the US Coastguard just days before it was due to sail. Crise was forced to find an alternative boat but that cost an extra $30,000.

The final stroke of misfortune occurred when a driver was seriously injured during the Nassau Trophy Race. The Ferrari driven by Rodrigo Borjes Zingg flipped over after hitting a safety fence and caught fire.

There were some unusual car and engine combinations at Nassau, including the MGA-Jaguar of Nassau resident James O'Connor. He managed to finish in 4th place in the 12-lap Bahamas Cup Race.
(John Owen. Terry O'Neil Collection)

Demonstrating the dexterity which made him the world's third top driver of 1966, Austria's Jochen Rindt guides his Austro Vau to record-time first place money in the Formula Vee Grand Prix of Volkswagens. The young Austrian led his Austro Vau team to the first three places in the 100-mile race. (Bahamas Ministry of Tourism. Terry O'Neil Collection)

Race starter Arch James surveys the field for the first heat of the Ladies' Race. The competitors all borrowed Formula Vees from other drivers to take part in the event. The heat winner, Ms D Carter, started from the fifth row of the grid. Patsy Kenedy finished in second place and Janet Guthrie third. (Bahamas Ministry of Tourism. Terry O'Neil Collection)

Pedro Rodriguez drove a Ferrari 275GTB/C in the combined Nassau Tourist Trophy and Governor's Trophy Race, finishing in 6th place overall, 1st in Class 12GT. (John Owen. Terry O'Neil Collection)

Anita Taylor was spending her honeymoon in the Bahamas at the time of the Speed Weeks. She tried her luck in both the Governor's Trophy and Nassau Trophy Races driving the Ring Free Oil-sponsored Ford Mustang. Anita gained a creditable 15th overall place in the Nassau Trophy Race against some formidable opposition. (John Owen. Terry O'Neil Collection)

This is the view that all drivers were most familiar with of Sharp's Chaparral during the combined Nassau Tourist Trophy and Governor's Trophy Race. He drove away from the remainder of the field with consummate ease, lapping everyone to win the race. Brett Lunger finished in second place and Richard Brown in third place, both driving McLarens. (John Owen. Terry O'Neil Collection)

Well out-classed but enjoying themselves, drivers of the smaller capacity cars fought for Class honours. The Porsche 911 of Anton von Dory gained 2nd in Class 9GT in the Nassau Trophy Race, while the Matra Gordini driven by Howard Hanna failed to finish the race. (John Owen. Terry O'Neil Collection)

Fresh from early Cam-Am exploits AJ Foyt drove the Lola T70 to victory in the 4-lap Nassau Classic sprint. The car failed to impress in the Nassau Trophy Race, going out on lap 22. (John Owen. Terry O'Neil Collection)

Peter Gregg's Porsche Carrera 6 put up a commendable fight to finish in 8th place in the Nassau Trophy Race. Skip Scott's McLaren has just lapped him on his way to finish in second place in the race. (John Owen. Terry O'Neil Collection)

Mark Donohue (#7) and Hap Sharp (#65) had Chevrolet engines in their cars, and the evenly matched cars kept close formation until the final lap of the race when Sharp's car went out of control and crashed. It later came to light that Donohue was using a secret fuel tank on his Lola, which explained the rapid mandatory pit stop of 7.5 seconds. He finished the race just 4.5 seconds ahead of Skip Scott in a McLaren M1-B. (Bahamas Ministry of Tourism. Terry O'Neil Collection)

Part of the reward of winning the featured Nassau Trophy Race for Mark Donohue was the special attention he received from Liz Frink of Dusseldorf, the newly crowned Miss Bahamas International of 1966. Mark Donohue from New York became the first to claim the Oakes Memorial Trophy, presented after the death of Sir Sydney Oakes, with his down-to-the-wire finish in the 252 mile event. (Bahamas Ministry of Tourism. Terry O'Neil Collection)

Zingg was pulled out of the car alive, but he died later in a Florida hospital.

The Volkswagen Grand Prix was won by Jochen Rindt, and the combined Nassau Tourist Trophy and Governor's Trophy Race by Hap Sharp in a Chaparral. Mark Donohue drove his Lola T70 to victory in the Nassau Trophy Race at a record speed of 105.7mph.

Early in 1967 it became apparent that no more money would be forthcoming from the Development Board, and Red Crise begrudgingly acknowledged that the days of the Speed Weeks were numbered. The races appeared to have an insatiable appetite for devouring large amounts of money, and without it there could be no event. The final nail in the coffin for Crise was a change in government in the Bahamas, as the Progressive Liberal Party took control. It had long advocated against holding the Speed Weeks, regarding the event as a waste of money.

On reflection, though, despite its shortcomings, one can say that the event achieved the effect that the Development Board had initially hoped for, i.e. developing tourism to the Bahamas. The tourism season had been extended by three months and the hotels were booming, this factor ironically contributing to Crise's problems, as he found he no longer had the bargaining power with the Hotel Association to acquire free accommodation for the race drivers.

Motor racing would be poorer for the loss of this glamorous, if somewhat eccentric, event that had brought the cream of the sports car driving talent to the Bahamas shores for thirteen years.

While there was a diverse mix of races staged throughout the thirteen years of the Speed Weeks, the winners of the two feature races held each year are shown in the following tables.

Summary of winners

The Governor's Cup Race

Year	Driver	Car	Distance (miles)	Time	Speed (mph)
1954 *	A De Portago	Ferrari 750 Monza	105	75m 08s	86.4
1955	A De Portago	Ferrari 750 Monza	105	68m 11s	92.4
1956 u	H Hively	Ferrari 500 TR	70	45m 05s	92.2
1956 o	C Shelby	Ferrari 410 Sport	70	42m 42s	99.1
1957 u	E Crawford	Porsche 550A	75	44m 58s	100.1
1957 o	P Hill	Ferrari 335S	75	43m 19s	103.9
1958	L Reventlow	RA-1 Scarab	112.5	76m 08s	88.6
1959 u	R Holbert	Porsche 718 RSK	54	37m 05s	87.5
1959 o	S Moss	Aston-Martin DBR2	54	35m 57s	90.1
1960	R Rodriguez	Ferrari 250TR 59	112.5	75m 34s	89.3
1961	P Rodriguez	Ferrari 250 TRI/61	103.5	69m 27s	89.4
1962	H Sharp	Cooper Monaco	76.5	50m 06s	91.6
1963	A J Foyt	Scarab Mk IV	112.5	69m 34s	97.0
1964	R Penske	Chaparral II	112.5	67m 25s	100.1
1965	B McLaren	McLaren M1-B	112.5	64m 31s	104.6
1966	H Sharp	Chaparral 2E	112.5	64m 53s	104.0

* The Bahamas Automobile Cup
u Under 2-litre cars
o Over 2-litre cars

The Nassau Trophy Race

Year	Driver	Car	Distance (miles)	Time	Speed (mph)
1954	M Gregory	Ferrari 375MM	210	141m 33s	89.2
1955	P Hill	Ferrari 857 Monza	210	130m 14s	98.2
1956	S Moss	Maserati 300S	210	130m 57s	96.2
1957	S Moss	Ferrari 290MM	250	147m 38s	101.6
1958	L Reventlow C Daigh	RA-1 Scarab	252	172m 18s	87.6
1959	G Constantine	Aston Martin DBR2	220.5	151m 37s	87.2
1960	D Gurney	Lotus XIX	243	162m 49s	89.5
1961	D Gurney	Lotus XIX	247.5	163m 33s	90.8
1962	I Ireland	Lotus XIX	252	179m 47s	84.1
1963	A J Foyt	Scarab Chev Mk IV	252	158m 31s	95.4
1964	H Sharp R Penske	Chaparral II	252	186m 20s	89.1
1965	H Sharp	Chaparral II AC	252	146m 24s	103.3
1966	M Donohue	Lola T70 Mk II	252	143m 04s	105.7

Also from Veloce Publishing –

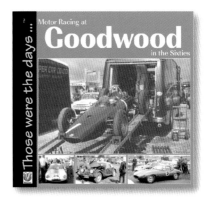

ISBN 9781903706497 • £12.99*

ISBN 9781903706817 • £9.99*

ISBN 9781903706015 • £9.99*

ISBN 9781903706794 • £9.99*

ISBN 9781903706886 • £12.99*

ISBN 9781904788959 • £12.99*

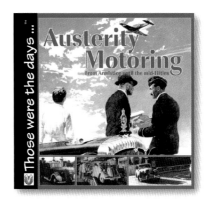

ISBN 9781903706862 • £9.99*

ISBN 9781904788065 • £12.99*

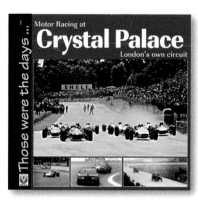

ISBN 9781904788348 • £12.99*

ISBN 9781845841140 • £12.99*

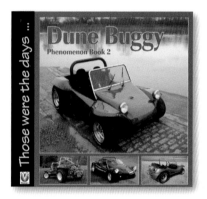

ISBN 9781904788669 • £12.99*

ISBN 9781845840389 • £12.99*

ISBN 9781845841645 • £12.99*

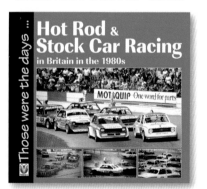

ISBN 9781845841676 • £12.99*

– with more to come!

Index

Cars

Abarth Simca 1300
    Bialbao 72
AC 37, 81
Alfa Romeo Giulietta 42,
    55
Allard J2 9
Aston-Martin 26, 35, 36,
    39
Austin-Healey 9, 16, 36,
    38, 41, 42, 45, 49, 72
Austro Vau FV 86
Autodynamics FV 85

Beach FV 80, 81, 85
BMW 72
Brabham 69

Chaparral 66, 75, 84, 88
Chevrolet Corvette 19,
    20, 23, 32, 34
Chevrolet Grand Sport
    62, 66, 70, 72
Cooper Monaco 59, 61,
    68, 75
Cooper T52 44

D B Panhard 28, 56, 58

Elva Mk3 75

Ferrari 250 GT 45, 58
Ferrari 250 GTO 54, 56,
58, 62
Ferrari 250 LM 69, 72
Ferrari 250 TR 29, 46,
    61
Ferrari 275 GTB/C 78,
    87
Ferrari 290MM 24
Ferrari 375MM 9
Ferrari 750 Monza 14
Ferrari 860 Monza 19,
    20
Ferrari Dino 37, 51
Fiat Abarth Zagato 32
Ford Falcon 54
Ford Galaxie 54, 57
Ford GT40 72, 73, 76
Ford Mustang 87

Genie-Chevrolet 75

Hussein Dodge Zerex
    Special 70, 72

Jaguar XK120 8, 12, 18,
    50

Lester-MG 13
Lola Mk6 GT 62, 63, 66
Lola T70 88, 90
Lotus 11 31, 72
Lotus 19 46, 47, 52, 59,
    61
Lotus 20 49
Lotus 40 81

Maserati 300S 20, 48

Maserati 450S 23, 30,
    40
Maserati Tipo 61 39,
    40, 52
Maserati Tipo 63 51
McLaren M1B 82, 89
MGA 25
MGB GT 78
MG TF 12

OSCA 1600 GT 55

PBX-Crosley 10
Porsche 356 17, 36, 59,
    80
Porsche Abarth 356B 61
Porsche 550 Spyder 23,
    24, 29
Porsche 718 RSK 35,
    37, 80
Porsche 904 GTS 78
Porsche 911 88

Renault Alpine 71

Sadler 31
Scarab 30, 32, 64, 66
Shelby Cobra 54, 62,
    68, 70
Shelby King Cobra 77
Singer 1500 9

VW FV 65, 66
VW GT 65

Race drivers

Ackerley, A 78
Albury, D 18, 42
Andrey, G 39, 40
Ash, D 12, 25

Baker, C 72
Bandini, L 56
Bethell, H 42
Black, D 13
Blanchard, H 37
Bonnier, J 27
Brown, H 39
Brundage, J 17

Cassell, C 61
Collins, J 37
Connell, A 52
Constantine, G 35
Crawford, E 23, 30
Cuevas, J 35, 36

Daigh, C 26, 30, 32
De Portago, A 13, 14,
    18, 19, 21, 23
Dieringer, D 57
Donohue, M 49, 89, 90

Easey, W 72

Fernandez, J 9, 13
Fleming, T 55, 72
Forbes, D 12
Foyt, A J 64, 66, 70, 72,
    88

Gammino, M 62, 65
Goldschmidt, E 9
Goldsmith, P 75
Gordon, J 80
Gregg, P 78, 89
Gregory, M 13, 14, 19, 23
Grossman, R 69, 81
Gurney, D 46, 47

Habersin, A 41
Hall, J 66, 84
Hanna, H 28, 58
Hayes, C 58, 82
Heppenstall, R 28, 68, 72
Hill, P 18, 19, 23, 76
Hitchcock, T 69
Hively, H 20
Holbert, R 63, 68
Hudson, S 75
Hugus, E 27, 78
Humphries 44

Ireland, I 61, 65

Jackson-Moore, R 16
Jeffords, J 32, 34

Kenedy, P 18, 50, 53, 59, 61, 80
Kolb, C 66, 81, 82

Levy, R 23, 24
Lollabrigida, G 48
Lovely, P 47, 49

Martin, E 29
Mayer, T 38
McLaren, B 76, 79, 81, 82
McCluggage, D 23, 31
Miles, K 70
Moore, K 32
Moss, S 16, 19, 20, 24, 26, 35, 39, 44, 45, 47, 52

Nethercutt, J 52, 59

Oakes, G 11, 16, 20, 30, 61
Oakes, S 10, 11, 15, 16, 42, 85
O'Connor, J 86

Pabst, A 62, 63, 66
Payne, T 65, 81, 82
Penske, R 49, 61, 70, 84
Pigott, P 49
Poole, C 10

Reed, G 61
Reventlow, L 26, 30, 32
Rindt, J 86, 90
Rodriguez, P 29, 37, 47, 54, 72, 87
Rodriguez, R 24, 25, 29, 34, 46, 54
Ruby, L 40, 59

Said, B 31
Saunders, J 43, 70

Schechter, R 37, 53
Schenk, H 38, 80
Schmidt, O 33, 66
Scott, S 89
Sharp, H 61, 75, 84, 88, 89, 90
Shelby, C 19, 20, 26, 40

Taylor, A 87
Turner, C 23

Vaccarella, N 51

Waltman, G 17

Zingg, R 86

Races, teams, establishments, officials
American Automobile Association 5, 8

Bahamas Automobile Club 5, 27
Bahamas Development Board 5, 35, 77, 9
British Colonial Hotel 8

Crise S 'Red' 4, 5, 18, 20, 27, 43, 66, 69, 77, 79, 85, 90

Esso Standard Oil 22

Hillcrest House 20

James A 54, 68, 87

Lake Cunningham 20

Mecom J 63, 72
Mecom Team 63, 70

North American Racing Team 47, 54, 65

Oakes Course 22, 27
Oakes Field 22

Pan-American F J 43, 44, 47, 59
Progressive Liberal Party 35, 77, 90

Rosebud Team 47, 65
Royal Automobile Association 5

Scuderia Serenissima 47
Sports Car Club of America (SCCA) 5, 27

United Bahamian Party 77
United States Automobile Club 27

Windsor Field 4, 7